Divine Covenant

from
Victim to Victory

T. F. Hoskins

Printed and bound in the United States of America
10 9 8 7 6 5 4 3 2 1

First edition - 2017
Creative Direction: T.F. Hoskins and Tamiko Lowry-Pugh,
Author Writer Services
Cover Photo: T.F. Hoskins

ISBN-13: 978-0692892480

DEDICATION

I dedicate this devotional to my late brother who some affectionately referred to as KC or Big K. You are greatly missed by me and all those who had the pleasure of knowing you. There are days when I can still see your smile; those infectious smiles that caused your eyes to disappear. I have yet to meet a person who can smile that hard. Although there is still pain from your absence, know that I love you and forgive you for leaving us too soon. I release you from the bondage of my unanswered questions. Fly high my brother, fly high.

K.B.C
Sunrise 11/16/1986 ~ Sunset 4/30/2011

Your story lives on **;** Take these broken wings and learn to fly.

#SuicidePrevetion
#ChooseLife
#V2V

ACKNOWLEDGEMENT

I thank God for keeping me in my right mind during my darkest moments and for giving me the courage to be transparent with my challenges. I pray this work honors You by unveiling some of the common lies I believed. I pray this journey will continue to free any strongholds within me.

To my family; blood relatives and my chosen family by way of marriage and friendships. Each of you have allowed me to see God's presence through our interaction. You have fed my soul in countless ways; you've loved me, supported me, challenged me and stretched me in ways I didn't think were possible. I am the woman I am today because of who you have been to me. I thank you and love you to life. Your date of births were used to thank each of you in a special way for giving me life.

Lastly, but certainly not least, I thank you for reading this book and journeying through our challenges together. I hope we will be able to lovingly encourage each other through life's challenges. You are not alone.

Supporting Companies

John Carpenter, Christian Counselor-League of Lions, LLC
Kimberly Renay Consulting
Lewis Blake Consulting – Commercial Credit
Pragmatic Financial Strategies, Inc.
Season of Preparation
TriCloud Communications
Tamiko Lowry–Pugh Author/Writer Services

CONTENTS

INTRODUCTION

I imagine you are thinking this is a memoir of how people hurt me and how I was able to overcome those disappoints. Surprise! This is actually my truth about the unnecessary pain I have inflicted upon myself by doubting God's promises. The past few years of my life brought serious circumstances my way, and my spirit became weak. It became easy for the enemy to attack my mind, and I subconsciously accepted defeat in every situation. I truly believed the lies, I was the tail and not the head, and I developed a culture of accepting less. Accepting mediocrity for my life subconsciously gave me permission to devalue the people I love as God has called me to love them. God is not pleased with the fruit of "less than." A mindset of mediocrity cannot coexist with a Kingdom lifestyle.

The truth is, I don't have the answers. I don't have a magic wand or the solutions to your issues (the real ones or the ones you've conjured up in your mind). Your answers rest within God, coupled with your desire and ability to hear from Him. God is constantly guiding us, so listen! My sole purpose for this book is to support you through your journey; your journey to live in God's truth and not in the fallacies of this world.

As we begin our journey together, may I suggest you allot 10 minutes out of the 1,440 minutes in a day? I intentionally kept each day short to help us create a habit of meditating on His word *every* day. I believe as we master the 10-minute exercises, our spirits will require more time with God and we will begin to schedule more time to consume His Word. Here are some simple recommendations to make this journey a successful transformation.

1) Designate a convenient time every day. I would recommend that you set your alarm 10 minutes early every morning.
2) Turn off all background noise and any potential distractions.

9

3) Pray. Asking God to illuminate what He wants you to see in each scripture. It takes only 2 minutes to read each day.
4) Take notes and list your statement of confession. This is extremely important to personalize your statement based on the scripture. Even if you believe your confession aligns with my point of view, reiterate that in your statement of confession. Make it personal.
5) Use the hashtags on each page to connect with me and the community studying the devotional so we can support you through your journey.
6) Pray without ceasing. Even when you don't know the words to say or cannot remember the daily mantra, just call on His name. There is a glossary at the end of the book with the different names of God. Just call on His name.

Feel empowered to repeat any day as much as needed. It is not necessary to complete this devotional in 31 days. It is only imperative that you memorize/meditate on His word, purge the lies and hold on to His promises. I have held on to 1 scripture for the past 6 months, and it has been enough to pull me out of the abyss. There is a shift in the atmosphere, and it's time to hear His truth, walk in it and live. Make the conscious decision to stop merely existing, and live! It is my heart's desire to encourage you in your individual growth so you may foster healthy relationships and ultimately positively impact this world as you thrive within your family. Here's to our partnership as we hold each other accountable without judgment.

Day 1

And the Lord, He is the One who goes before you.
He will be with you, He will not leave you nor
forsake you; do not fear nor be dismayed.
Deuteronomy 31:8 NKJV

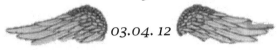 *03.04. 12*

MYTH: I have prayed and fasted and prayed and fast (place that on repeat), but my reality still has not changed. I hear Him clearly. I know I do, because I meditate on what I've heard, looked for contradiction in His word and can't find one. Prayed again, sought wise counsel, prayed some more, asked and received signs. In case you haven't noticed, I am relentless; persistence is a strong force in me! Despite all that, the results are the same. The challenge at hand still exists. God - are you listening? I am living in obedience, praying, fasting, and yet my world looks bleak. Why have You abandoned me? I have faced abandonment from loved ones, but this pain I feel from being abandoned by You is suffocating. Where are You when I need You? What have I done for You to forsake me?

#ThriveLife
#YouAreNotAlone
#V2V

TRUTH: God never left me. The very fact that I am writing this book in my right mind is testimony that He is here and still sovereign. I don't understand the pains I have felt, but I can attest that my pain has birthed something in me. Life exists only with God; therefore I know He has been with me through every process. The greatest proof of His presence is the spiritual and emotional transformation in me. I am a work in progress, but I am thankful He never gave up on me. Although I have a long way to go, my response to situations are changing, and I know it is not by my own strength.

MANTRA: Jehovah Shammah I thank You for being present even in the midst of my doubt.

Statement of Confession:

_____

_____

_____

_____

_____

_____

_____

_____

_____

_____

_____

_____

_____

_____

_____

_____

#ThriveLife
#YouAreNotAlone
#V2V

Day 2

When I was a child, I spoke as a child, I understood as a child, I thought as a child; but when I became a man, I put away childish things.
1 Corinthians 13:11 NKJV

 *11.16.82*

MYTH: The lie of entitlement. I have been having a real grown woman tantrum for the past...well, as long as I have been a woman actually. My tantrums have been for different reasons with different people, but they have been real. As a matter of fact; I still struggle in that area. To date; there is one particular situation I am still having a tantrum with. I am unable to control the outcome, and I am emotionally pouting, kicking and screaming all the way through the process. It's my truth. A truth I have to own so I can transition from having *all* my grown woman tantrums; *most* just won't do. As I said in my introduction, this is my truth and my willingness to partner with you as we weed through the lies of this world.

#ThriveLife
#NoMoreGrownupTantrums
#V2V

TRUTH: Life doesn't always pan out the way we hoped. Maturity is when you are able to process life's disappointments, harness the lessons, and continue to journey on without picking up the sorrow. When you travel with the sorrows from your disappointments, it prevents you from taking hold of the new blessings. Travel light.

MANTRA: Peleh Yo'etz, show me Your ways. Speak to my heart so that I may respond to disappointments with humility and not entitlement.

Statement of Confession:

_____

_____

_____

_____

_____

_____

_____

_____

_____

_____

_____

_____

_____

_____

_____

_____

_____

_____

#ThriveLife
#NoMoreGrownupTantrums
#V2V

Day 3

Do not say, "I will recompense evil"; Wait for the Lord, and He will save you.
Proverbs 20:22 NKJV

 03.01.60

MYTH: Seriously? Some people have the audacity to mistake kindness for weakness or silence for stupidity. Such misjudgment can bring out a destructive side. A side of me that seeks revenge and to re-educate them that I am not to be tampered with. Injustice activates an instinct to defend myself or anyone on the receiving end, and it can become confrontational. Although I prefer to avoid confrontation, I am not afraid to face it head on when needed. Initially, I will retreat, and if there are further offenses, I will suit up for battle. When I battle, I intend to win. This is the version of myself that concerns me. I lack mercy when I feel like I am being forced into a battle I want to avoid at all cost. Warrior verse humanitarian; I don't want to participate in this internal battle anymore.

#ThriveLife
#VengenceIsNotMine
#V2V

15

TRUTH: Vengeance is not a healthy response to injustice. Revenge only continues the cycle of wrongdoing and therefore feeds the monster of injustice. Release vengeance from your heart, it seeks to destroy everything in its path, even you. Anger, sorrow, disappointment, confusion are all emotions you can process and move past, but a vengeful spirit can result in permanent damage to you and all the people you love. As much as I may feel disdain for someone's actions, I know I have to release it, for my survival and ultimately to live in truth and love with my family and friends.

MANTRA: Jehovah Hashopet, I thank you for being just in all things. I can rest in knowing that your judgment will go forth.

Statement of Confession:

_____
_____
_____
_____
_____
_____
_____
_____
_____
_____
_____
_____
_____
_____
_____
_____
_____

#ThriveLife
#VengenceIsNotMine
#V2V

Day 4

For as by one man's disobedience many were made sinners, so also by one Man's obedience many will be made righteous.
Romans 5:19 NKJV

 *09.06.54*

MYTH: Somehow we've come to believe that being obedient will change our circumstance in a snap. We have convinced ourselves that obedience will somehow change the circumstances and the people around us in the way we hoped for. We make sacrifices and even withhold peace and ultimately joy from ourselves just to say we have been obedient, and to receive a certain response. I have been obedient out of obligation and guilt and have even fallen into the trap of being obedient simply to be an example for others. Acting obedient without an obedient heart has led to resentment.

#ThriveLife
#BoldObedience
#V2V

17

TRUTH: I had to accept that my obedience was not always pure. The root of our obedience is crucial. Obedience is necessary because our God calls us into obedience, that is the only reason required. Our reward of obedience is in eternal life. Yes, there are many blessings God grants us here on earth for being obedient, but it doesn't always look the way we envisioned. Stop being obedient to get a certain outcome from people or your circumstances! Be obedient only because He commands it and we seek to live the life He has called us to live. Our desire to please Him should be the reason we remain obedient. When we change our why, we free ourselves from being controlled by the results.

MANTRA: Adonai, I thank you for your son Jesus Christ as the perfect example of obedience and the Holy Spirit to guide me in my obedience.

Statement of Confession:

_____

_____

_____

_____

_____

_____

_____

_____

_____

_____

_____

_____

_____

_____

#ThriveLife
BoldObedience
#V2V

Day 5

*And now abide faith, hope, love, these three; but
the greatest of these is love
I Corinthians 13:13 NKJV*

 *07.16.80*

MYTH: I feel cheated. My heart is full of love for others, and my intentions are good. I truly desire to bless others and do my very best by each person, but I often question if that has brought me pain. The moments where I have experienced my deepest pains were caused by people I love, people I would go without for so that they will have. That kind of pain has threatened to change the core of my being. In order not to change, I have developed the habit of retreating; I pull away from whoever/whatever is causing pain. It has caused isolation and often spiraled into a victim mentality of feeling sorry for myself. Usually, that will last a while, and my thoughts about love and being loved seem impossible.

#ThriveLife
#ContinueToLove
#V2V

TRUTH: Because I am also seeking God; especially in my isolation and brokenness, my retreat always end when I hear, "Don't change your ability and desire to love deeply! Out of that pain, continue to love, continue to forgive, continue to grow, never let bitterness in. That pain was not meant for you, when you hurt, I hurt. When you are broken, you resist being used by Me. Continue to love and love more abundantly, and this is how you will remind others of Who I Am; love unconditionally."

MANTRA: Elohei Chasdi, I welcome You to be Lord of all my emotions, strengthen me to extend Your love to others.

Statement of Confession:

_____
_____
_____
_____
_____
_____
_____
_____
_____
_____
_____
_____
_____
_____
_____
_____
_____
_____
_____

#ThriveLife
#ContinueToLove
#V2V

Day 6

I, even I, am He who blots out your transgressions for My own sake; And I will not remember your sins.
Isaiah 43:25 NKJV

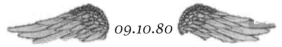 09.10.80

MYTH: That moment you realize that you have also hurt someone you love; it can cripple you. Although unintentional, when I become aware of the pain I have caused, the sadness is even heavier than when someone hurts me. In that moment, my pain has often been greater than the pain I inflicted. That sorrow can cause me to sink. I begin to believe that I am unworthy of love, unworthy of even being liked and unworthy of being trusted. The destruction of these lies of unworthiness only leads to more self-destructive and unloving behaviors. Falling into this cycle of lies is almost impossible to break because I begin to own an identity that does not reflect who I am.

#ThriveLife
#IForgiveMyself
#V2V

TRUTH: My reality is, I've hurt people I love because I failed to deal with past pains. When I realize my afflictions, I always repent in my quiet time with God, seek forgiveness from the person I've hurt, and try to forgive myself. Forgiving myself is always the hardest part of the process. You would think forgiving myself was easy because I knew my intentions were pure. But, it can be hard to release the guilt when my reflections reveal that I missed all the cues that my behaviors were potentially hurtful. I missed the caution signs because of my inflated sense of being emotionally in tune. Pride prevented me from seeing clearly.

MANTRA: Jehovah Goelekh, You believe I am worthy of forgiveness, help me to forgive myself as You've forgiven me.

Statement of Confession:

_____
_____
_____
_____
_____
_____
_____
_____
_____
_____
_____
_____
_____
_____
_____
_____

#ThriveLife
#IForgiveMyself
#V2V

Day 7

Be anxious for nothing, but in everything by prayer and supplication, with thanksgiving, let your requests be made known to God
Philippians 4:6 NKJV

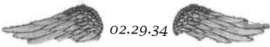 02.29.34

MYTH: Here I am again, worrying! These thoughts can be maddening. Constantly operating from a place of fear is not of God, it results in impulsive behaviors that can jeopardize the end goal. This worry/fear cycle is all my fault. Instead of consuming the Word and meditating on God's instructions, I gave the enemy screen time in my mind. I allowed the enemy to play every character in all the scenarios in my mind. There is no space for light. Before I can complete a positive thought, he steals that possibility of hope. Snatched it right out of my heart and mind - then I spiral into thoughts of defeat.

#ThriveLife
#DoNotWorry
#V2V

TRUTH: Stop! Stop! Stop! When worry comes (and it will come), stop it from taking over by finding a mantra for that moment, that day, even if it is the same mantra you hold onto for a year. Hold on and put it on repeat. Say it out loud if you must. Saying it quietly can be tricky, the enemy has a way of causing your thoughts to drift, so say it out loud in front of the mirror until you begin to know. Know the truth, you are greater than, know the truth that you are the head and not the tail. Know that God will provide all of your needs and many of your wants. Look at your life; He already has!

MANTRA: Jehovah Jireh will provide more than I need.

Statement of Confession:

_____

_____

_____

_____

_____

_____

_____

_____

_____

_____

_____

_____

_____

_____

_____

_____

#ThriveLife
#DoNotWorry
#V2V

Day 8

And the peace of God, which surpasses all
understanding, will guard your hearts and
minds through Christ Jesus.
Philippians 4:7 NKJ

 06.09.50

MYTH: Noise! Outside of Sunday and Thursday evenings when I have corporate fellowship at church, every day seems hectic. I want to run and hide sometimes. I am a runner. I actually day dream of going off the grid; no phone, no internet, no television, no family, no friends, I don't even want many of my thoughts there either. If I had a switch, it would be lights out on these thoughts! All I want some days is God and the wonders of nature. As much as I love music, I don't even want man made music. The natural sound of nature itself would be enough melody for my soul. Where can I go to shut the world out, center my mind and refocus on Him and His plan for my life?

#ThriveLife
#LordGrantMeYourPeace
#V2V

25

TRUTH: We have a specific space for everything, the place we cook, eat, sleep, bathe, but there is no designated space to worship; this seemed backwards to me. How can we not have a designated space to worship God in our homes when He blessed us with a home? So, I got to work! I don't need to go off the grid! I just created a designated space for prayer, meditation, and worship in the Northeast section of my home. My worship nook was one of the best things I could do. Let's face it, although your entire home should be your sanctuary, sometimes we want to run and hide even within our homes. My worship nook is my quiet place where I am learning the art of silencing the world and listening to God.

MANTRA: Jehovah Shalom quench my mind, heart, and soul with Your rivers of peace and silence.

Statement of Confession:

_____
_____
_____
_____
_____
_____
_____
_____
_____
_____
_____
_____
_____
_____
_____

#ThriveLife
#LordGrantMeYourPeace
#V2V

Day 9

Surely every man walks about like a shadow;
Surely they busy themselves in vain; He heaps
up riches, and does not know who will gather
them.
Psalms 39:6 NKJV

 04.06.99

MYTH: I am always ripping and running and feeling like there is not enough time in the day. I feel like I am always going and yet nothing is getting done except wear and tear on my body. I am exhausted, and yet I have not made any progress in what God set aside for me to do. Somehow I have managed to grind for my employer and whatever organization I am volunteering with at the moment. I execute all the tasks my employer directs me to complete for the day and some days, even more. I have even completed tasks my employer expects my cohorts to complete. Why? What am I trying to prove and who am I trying to please? Resentment is growing because I am burning the candle from both ends. My best feels like it's not good enough for anyone or anything. So I overcompensate in every area of my life only to fall short in every area of my life.

#ThriveLife
#MyBestIsGoodEnough
#V2V

27

TRUTH: My best is good enough! My best is good enough for each day God blesses me to see. I don't have to produce my parents', my husband's, my son's, my brothers' or anyone else's best. God only requires our best every day, and He will take care of the rest. My loved ones never asked me to compensate for their lack, and they don't want me to either. When I overcompensate for their lack, subconsciously I make them feel like I don't believe in their ability or desire to give their best. Sadly, when they do give their best, my overcompensation subconsciously says to them that their best isn't enough for me.

MANTRA: Elohim Ozer Li, my best is good enough today, and I am free for my best to look different each day. Thank you for helping me where I may lack.

Statement of Confession:

_____
_____
_____
_____
_____
_____
_____
_____
_____
_____
_____
_____
_____
_____
_____
_____
_____

#ThriveLife
#MyBestIsGoodEnough
#V2V

Day 10

But indeed for this purpose I have raised you up, that I may show My power in you, and that My name may be declared in all the earth.
Exodus 9:16 NKJV

 08.22.78

MYTH: Depleted, that is how I feel. Who do I have to blame for that but myself? It is a blessing to serve others, but not at the capacity where you've depleted your energy at levels that take you off course. There is a clear difference between being tired versus depleted. When you are depleted, you are distracted and your zeal to walk in your true purpose becomes a memory. I am guilty of getting distracted with good deeds that prevent me from executing the great deeds God has called me to. I am only serving my ego when I tire myself out with tasks that cause me to be weary. I am not even purely serving the people I do the good deeds for because I am not 100% present. Therefore, how is my mediocrity serving God?

#ThriveLife
#ConsultGodInAllThings
#V2V

TRUTH: Use your energy wisely. Get into your quiet space and seek God's guidance on who, where and how He would have you serve. More than likely, you have discussed opportunities to serve with a family member and or friends, so why have you not asked God? He knows all. If your desire is truly to please God, you will seek His guidance in the most mundane tasks. When you make a daily habit of consulting God, you will train your heart and your ear to hear Him and when it's time to consult Him on the chess-like moves in your life; "easy peasy lizard squeezy."

MANTRA: Peleh Yo'etz, order my steps in this day to serve as You see fit.

Statement of Confession:

_____

_____

_____

_____

_____

_____

_____

_____

_____

_____

_____

_____

_____

_____

_____

_____

_____

#ThriveLife
#ConsultGodInAllThings
#V2V

Day 11

Do not turn to idols, nor make for yourselves
molded gods: I am the Lord your God.
Leviticus 19:4 NKJV

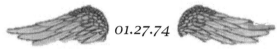 01.27.74

MYTH: Seriously? Really? Why have I not been able to find a solution and or fix things? Grrrr! I am wise and even have a good amount of street sense. I can read most people like a book. My discernment is almost always on point, and yet I can't figure this out. In this moment, I don't know if I am coming or going. This lack of know-how feels uncomfortable. I am like a fish out of water when I don't have a solution at my fingertips. Have I lost my intellectual swag? Who will figure this out or fix it if I can't? It doesn't seem like anyone else is qualified or even concerned enough for a solution. Am I the only one who realizes that there is an issue to be resolved?

#ThriveLife
#IntellectualSwagVersusSpiritualSwag
#V2V

TRUTH: Be very careful not to begin to view yourself as god. We are all tempted to be little gods in our own world because it is part of our nature. After all, we were created in God's very own image. Don't let the enemy use your spiritual DNA to give you a false sense of elevation. Always be mindful of your position, and posture yourself accordingly. Seeing yourself as a god will give you the false belief that your situations are limited to what you can accomplish versus what God is able to do. Who says you have to fix everything? Is God not more than qualified and capable to fix all things?

MANTRA: Jehovah Kanna Shemo, I submit all things to You and not the gods I have created. Forgive me.

Statement of Confession:

_____
_____
_____
_____
_____
_____
_____
_____
_____
_____
_____
_____
_____
_____
_____
_____
_____

#ThriveLife
#IntellectualSwagVersusSpiritualSwag
#V2V

Day 12

And the vision of the evenings and mornings Which was told is true; Therefore seal up the vision, For it refers to many days in the future.
Daniel 8:26 NKJV

 *12.10.85*

MYTH: It's 3am and I am awake - again. This has been happening for....well, over a year. Sleep, sweet sleep, please come to me? Awake worrying about matters I have no control over. Awake replaying events in my head, some great moments and some terrible ones. Awake being stuck between my past and what is to come. Awake, engaging in 3am eating sprints – yuck! When will my mind find rest? When will I rest? This worrying is screaming hypocrisy! I say I believe in God's divine Will and infinite ability, but yet I worry. I am stuck in the cycle of limiting my future based on my past joys and past pains. I am constantly looking in my rearview mirror. Crash!

#ThriveLife
#DontRearEndYourFuture
#V2V

TRUTH: I need to look forward before I rear-end my future! I almost totaled my present and my future because I was looking in my rearview mirror. My rearview mirror is there for reference only. Quickly look back for a reference point and place your eyes back on the windshield! How can you see where you are going if you are not looking through the windshield? Journey with wisdom of what you see spiritually! Use your spiritual wipers to clean off the debris from the storm, refuel and keep it pushing. Back on the road we go!

MANTRA: Today I release the bondage of my past and receive the blessings to come.

Statement of Confession:

_____
_____
_____
_____
_____
_____
_____
_____
_____
_____
_____
_____
_____
_____
_____
_____
_____
_____

#ThriveLife
#DontRearEndYourFuture
#V2V

Day 13

Restore to me the joy of Your Salvation, And uphold me by Your generous Spirit.
Psalms 51:12 NKJV

 11.20.89

MYTH: My joy has been displaced. My joy has been dependent on my status; my performance as a wife, mother, daughter, sister, friend, coworker (insert your labels), the list goes on. How can I find joy if I continue to place my joy in who I am to others? People constantly change, and so do their needs. I can't possibly sustain who I am to everyone. Why do I continue to place these unrealistic expectations on myself and expect favorable outcomes? Sometimes I wonder if I am an optimist at heart or simply a fool chasing dreams.

#ThriveLife
#EverlastingJoy
#V2V

TRUTH: I am not responsible for being everything to everyone I love. It is time to place my joy in God and He alone; I need the strength of the Holy Spirit to transform my natural inclination to be everything to everyone. The only status that should define my joy is my identity of being God's daughter! My salvation is enough to bring me joy every day despite my circumstances.

MANTRA: El Simchath Gili, my identity in You is enough.

Statement of Confession:

_____
_____
_____
_____
_____
_____
_____
_____
_____
_____
_____
_____
_____
_____
_____
_____
_____

#ThriveLife
#EverlastingJoy
#V2V

Day 14

Let all bitterness, wrath, anger, clamor and evil speaking be put away from you, with all malice.
Ephesians 4:31 NKJV

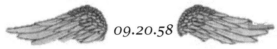 09.20.58

MYTH: I have sinned. I continue to spiral out of control. Cursing, displaying anger by yelling, saying extremely hurtful things I truly don't mean, sometimes I even shut down. There was a time in my life where violence and striking someone was the result of my anger. Now, I mostly shut down, and that is extremely toxic also, I become an incubator for defeating thoughts. When someone's actions cause me pain, I get angry at myself for trusting them and replay events to pinpoint signs that would have cautioned me not to trust. I am naturally inclined not to trust, so it's easy to find something, and then the anger is compounded. My anger is usually with myself for having good expectations from an interaction, and that is usually when the unhealthy responses come.

#ThriveLife
#FruitOfTheSpirit
#V2V

TRUTH: Vulnerability terrifies me. It takes a long time for me to trust someone enough to be vulnerable and let down my guard. I am thankful God has delivered me from the gripping bondage of violence, but most recently, I have used my mouth and manipulation as a weapon. Some of my response clearly indicate that there is some residual healing left. Feeling angry is okay, it is actually a natural human emotion when you feel deeply wronged. However, my responses to anger are still not healthy.

The truth is, truly loving someone is seeing and trusting the God in them even when they've hurt you. God, I ask for your mercy. Let me be slow to speak out of anger and eager to listen. Eager to learn what the experience is trying to teach.

MANTRA: Jehovah Tsemach, help me to respond to all situations with the fruit of Your Spirit and learn to trust the God in each person.

Statement of Confession:

_____
_____
_____
_____
_____
_____
_____
_____
_____
_____

#ThriveLife
#FruitOfTheSpirit
#V2V

Day 15

And do not be conformed to this world, but be transformed by the renewing of your mind, that you may prove what is that good and acceptable and perfect will of God.
Romans 12:2 NKJV

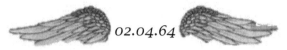 02.04.64

MYTH: I begin each day with such lofty dreams of what the day will hold. When this happens, I usually have flashbacks of the previous day, and just like that, the racing begins! Thoughts of what needs to be different in this day (which somehow automatically translates to "better" in my mind) consume me. What wasted brain power! Although it is responsible to set Godly goals and actively work towards them, obsessing over any goal will birth gods in our lives. Obsessive thoughts can hinder action and keep you in unproductive thought patterns.

#ThriveLife
#GodCenteredMind
#V2V

TRUTH: A mind that is spinning without direction is not a God-centered mind. Even when your mind is racing with thoughts pertaining to the areas in which God has called you to serve, it is unhealthy. God calls us to be about His business, not obsess about our busyness. Busyness to the point of feeling chronically drained and stretched thin over an extended period of time is not what God desires. The enemy will use busyness as a distraction to take your mind off Who (GOD) and why (advancing His Kingdom), and before you know it, your desire and ability to serve has exponentially decreased. The reality is, as long as we focus on God and actively live out our purpose(s), God will take care of the rest. He will supply all of our needs and many of our wants.

MANTRA: Elohim Ozer Li, today help me to trade my busyness to be about Your business.

Statement of Confession:

_____
_____
_____
_____
_____
_____
_____
_____
_____
_____
_____

#ThriveLife
#GodCenteredMind
#V2V

Day 16

So the Lord alone led him, And there was no foreign god with him.
Deuteronomy 32:12 NKJV

 2.26.55

MYTH: There are so many big decisions to be made. I am overwhelmed, and I am afraid of making the wrong decisions because these decisions are life changing. What should I do? When I am in my quiet time with God, I hear "Be still." It is downright scary for people with my personality not to have a clear answer. The control of knowing, whether good or bad, brings more comfort than a positive unknown. Knowing gives me permission to move in my own ability and independent of anyone. I am addicted to knowing because it gives me the "feeling" that I am in control of my own destiny.

#ThriveLife
#GuideMeLord
#V2V

TRUTH: Stillness is a huge challenge for my personality make up. It's a challenge because there are never details that come with being still. What I have learned, is stillness lacks details to prevent the temptation to act on my own will. The details of why, how, how long and what's at the end, are often missing when you are asked to be still. Some of my greatest lessons have been learned in my stillness, and I am learning to seek God for guidance on all decisions (big and small) before I move. I thirst for His guidance. It is not easy, but I am learning to be still and rest until clearly hearing from God.

Learn to rest in your quiet time with Him.

MANTRA: Peleh Yo'etz, I release my desire to control the outcome. I will be still and lean into You and not my limited understanding.

Statement of Confession:

_____
_____
_____
_____
_____
_____
_____
_____
_____
_____
_____
_____
_____

#ThriveLife
#GuideMeLord
#V2V

Day 17

May the Lord answer you when you are in distress; may the name of the God of Jacob protect you.
Psalm 20:1 NIV

 *09.16.72*

MYTH: Today I hope to close my eyes, and God will allow me to rest forever. To drift off to eternity to finally experience what true bliss is; heaven! I have never contemplated suicide, but I don't want to feel any of my emotions anymore. I don't want to cry another tear. I want my reality of this suffocating pain to vanish. Why am I here God? Don't You see my anguish? There are some days that I begin to believe that God doesn't love me enough to save me from my pain. Clearly.....I am consumed with hopelessness. I can't see the light at the end of the tunnel. The further I travel down this tunnel the darker it gets.

#ThriveLife
#GodProtectMyMind
#V2V

TRUTH: The truth is, God loves you beyond your imagination. His love exceeds your human capacity to feel or to understand. In fact, God feels pain and sorrow when we hurt. God may have you in this place of anguish as protection. I know, how can pain be protection? Often times our temporary pain can stop us from a lifetime penalty. Our God will withhold a mediocre desire to bless us beyond what we imagined.

MANTRA: Elohe Yakob I know You are present and will protecting me all the days of my life.

Statement of Confession:

_____
_____
_____
_____
_____
_____
_____
_____
_____
_____
_____
_____
_____
_____
_____
_____
_____
_____
_____
_____

#ThriveLife
#GodProtectMyMind
#V2V

Day 18

Remember His covenant forever, The word which He commanded, for a thousand generations.
I Chronicles 16:15 NKJV

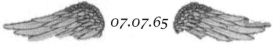 07.07.65

MYTH: Weary! My soul is weary. Before I can recover from one challenge, I am hit with another, and so it goes. This has been the case for an extended period of time now. Honestly, I am tired of disappointments. Some days I feel like my world is falling apart and it's even more discouraging to see most of the people I love in the same cycle. My prayer list is getting longer, and I can't seem to cross any items off the list as answered prayers. It would be really encouraging to have just 1 month where we are not staring a Goliath-size challenge in the face; the battle is exhausting.

#ThriveLife
#FocusOnHisPromises
#V2V

TRUTH: Weariness is a distraction to shift your focus off God's promises to the problem(s) you face. When life's challenges begin to compound, and you begin to feel overwhelmed, it is extremely important to hold onto God's promises. Write it down, say it out loud – daily if you have to. Any challenge you face is merely a task that needs to be dealt with temporarily. My life coach cautioned me during one of our sessions to stop focusing on who I don't want to be, and focus on the woman I aspire to be. He told me to be intentional about my vision because our brains do not effectively process negatives; our brains process commands. If your daily thoughts are, "don't be lazy," your brain will focus on laziness. Your brain requires your affirmation. If you don't want to be lazy, command "be productive." Shift your focus to affirm your promises.

MANTRA: El Emunah, I will set my eyes on You and focus on Your promises.

Statement of Confession:

_____

_____

_____

_____

_____

_____

_____

_____

_____

_____

_____

#ThriveLife
#FocusOnHisPromises
#V2V

Day 19

*Lord, I cry out to You; Make haste to me! Give
ear to my voice when I cry out to You.
Psalms 141:1 NKJV*

 08.13.84

MYTH: Irritable; that pretty much sums up my mood. I feel
like nothing is going as planned and I am misunderstood by
everyone. I feel like adulting is not working out well for me.
I don't want to be mature when all I want to do is cry and
have another grown woman tantrum (shaking my head).
Maybe if I cried long enough, all of my tears would be gone,
and I will never cry again. I hate crying. I really do. Crying
simply feels unnatural, spilling my pain all over my face and
onto my chest. I feel weak when I realize that my pain is
cascading onto my face. That's when the reality hits me, I
can no longer hide.

#ThriveLife
#AdultingIsToughStuff
#V2V

TRUTH: Bottling up your emotions is not healthy. Suppressing all your emotions turns you into a walking pressure-cooker. I realized suppressing has been a major contributor to my unhealthy emotional responses. When you stuff a multitude of emotions away without dealing with them, you limit your ability to direct how they come out when they begin to overflow. The key is to digest and deal with emotional stuff as it comes up, then dispose of it. What are you holding onto the hurt for? Who told you that hurt was non-perishable? Discard hurt before it's way past its shelf life and rots all your good fruit.

MANTRA: El Rai, please see me in my place of need today.

Statement of Confession:

_____

_____

_____

_____

_____

_____

_____

_____

_____

_____

_____

_____

_____

_____

_____

_____

#ThriveLife
#AdultingIsToughStuff
#V2V

Day 20

in hope of eternal life which God, who cannot lie, promised before time began,
Titus 1:2 NKJV

 06.19.88

MYTH: Lies! I have been lied to and lied about. There are so many lies floating around. Lies people have told about me, the lies Satan tells me about myself and the lies I am starting to believe about myself. The sweetest lies are the ones that keep me in a state of denial to protect me from painful realities. There are so many lies, I am actually starting to believe maybe God also lied to me about His promises. I am being devoured by these fallacies, and my spirit is gasping for one breath of truth.

#ThriveLife
#ThouShaltNotLie
#V2V

49

TRUTH: People lie, but we put so much weight on people's words. God is the only constant truth Who never lies! Whenever lies threaten to cloud your discernment, drive deeper in His word. He will always illuminate truth in the very area you need. His word has been constant since before the beginning of time, and there is no subject that is not plainly addressed in His word. Read and find the truth on your own. If your reality is different from His word, you can rest assured, that what you see before you, is a lie from the enemy. Be intentional in seeking God's truth daily so that you will not be tempted to believe the lies of the world.

MANTRA: Jehovah El Emeth illuminate Your truth this day.

Statement of Confession:

_____
_____
_____
_____
_____
_____
_____
_____
_____
_____
_____
_____
_____
_____
_____
_____
_____
_____

#ThriveLife
#ThouShaltNotLie
#V2V

Day 21

Even so you, since you are zealous for spiritual gifts, let it be for the edification of the church that you seek to excel.
I Corinthians 14:12 NKJV

 10.25.52

MYTH: How can this be? I hear from You all the time. I've heard clearly for me and for those close to me. Now, I feel like I only hear for others and I no longer hear Your direction for my life. I don't hear a strategy I can comprehend for my life. Everything I hear for myself seems impossible. Have you taken my gift of discernment because I've used it for my own glory and not for Yours? Could it be that You have taken away one of my greatest blessings because it has made me a demigod in my own eyes? I long to hear Your voice! I long to feel that special connection where You and I can talk all day. God, I long to hear from You!

#ThriveLife
#LordMoldMe
#V2V

TRUTH: God didn't take my gift of discernment. I simply refuse to believe what I hear because life looks different from what I hear. Recently I realized the circumstances will not change because the circumstances are dependent on me changing. That was a real revelation. There are times when you need to take inventory of what's inside you and shake some things up, do some spring cleaning in the dead of winter. Prepare your emotional storehouse for the change you are praying for. Think about it, do you really want God to start granting grandiose blessings we are not equipped to handle? It will ultimately end in ruins. Ever thought of changing your prayer to "God change me?"

MANTRA: Elohim, create in me a new heart. Search me and purge what You have not authorized.

Statement of Confession:

_____
_____
_____
_____
_____
_____
_____
_____
_____
_____
_____
_____
_____
_____
_____
_____

#ThriveLife
#LordMoldMe
#V2V

Day 22

And God will wipe away every tear from their eyes; there shall be no more death, nor sorrow, not crying. There shall be no more pain, for the former things have passed away.
Revelations 21:4 NKJV

 10.12.86

MYTH: Loss. Over the past couple of years, I have lost so many loved ones in a relatively short timeframe. Death, after death. I even lost a child; an unexpected pregnancy that resulted in a miscarriage. Something happened the moment I knew God blessed me with life again. In that moment, I knew I wanted our child; I was terrified, but this child was already loved. When there was no heartbeat, no sign of life after conception, I questioned God. Why did You bless me with conception only to bring death? More death? Take me instead, please? There are days I still question the whole purpose of my season of loss. I don't want to lose another person I love, my heart can't take it.

#ThriveLife
#GainingAngels
#V2V

TRUTH: It was really hard to lose loved ones, but what I didn't realize was that I gained so many angels. There are days when I feel lost without my loved ones, and it feels impossible to carry on without them, but God grants me strength for each day in knowing that one day we will all be reunited without sin or sickness.

MANTRA: Elohei Ma'uzzi, give me Your strength. Thank you for blessing me with the opportunity to experience love with each person I've lost. Greater still, I thank you for the opportunity to reconnect with them some day in heaven.

Statement of Confession:

_____

_____

_____

_____

_____

_____

_____

_____

_____

_____

_____

_____

_____

#ThriveLife
#GainingAngels
#V2V

Day 23

*When my father and mother forsake me, Then
the Lord will take care of me.
Psalms 27:10 NKJV*

 01.09.78

MYTH: Abandonment can leave you feeling a host of
unhealthy emotions, but by far the most damaging for me is
the feeling of unworthiness and not being loved. The scars
of abandonment left my heart bruised and tender. The
slightest touch of familiarity can make it feel broken all over
again. This wounded heart is hiding behind this hard
skeleton, and I am afraid to emerge. I cling tightly to the
carcass because it allows me to lie to the world about my
heart.

#ThriveLife
#HealNotHide
#V2V

TRUTH: Lying to yourself and others about where you are emotionally will ultimately make you feel more abandonment. You begin to believe the lie that you truly are alone. That feeling is a result of you shutting your support system out with lies. People are unable to support you in an area they don't know exists. Inevitably, you've also abandoned yourself by denying your truth and denying yourself of the support you need. Break the cycle of abandonment by not abandoning your own needs; choose you!

MANTRA: Jehovah Shammah, I thank You for being there for me even when I am not.

Statement of Confession:

_____
_____
_____
_____
_____
_____
_____
_____
_____
_____
_____
_____
_____
_____

#ThriveLife
#HealNotHide
#V2V

Day 24

Mercy and truth preserve the king, And by lovingkindness he upholds his throne.
Proverbs 20:28 NKJV

 08.20.82

MYTH: Well!...They needed to know the truth right? They asked, so what was I supposed to do, lie? The devil is a liar, and I am not the devil, so I am going to shoot straight from the hip. I will tell you the truth if you ask and even when you don't sometimes (that good old unsolicited advice... ha!). My family and friends know not to ask me something if they don't want to get the raw deal. My delivery has sometimes been curt and downright hurtful. Some may say, well, the truth hurts and if you are not willing to receive the truth, then don't ask.

#ThriveLife
#Truth
#V2V

Truth: They say the truth sets you free, but it can be distractingly hurtful when the delivery is not coming from a pure heart. My intentions are not pure when I deliver the truth in a careless way; my intentions are filled with forcing someone to deal with the truth, so I don't have to hear it, versus revealing the truth so that there can be healing. There are other times when I am simply frustrated because the truth is so obvious and I have witnessed the person denying it for so long. Such curt delivery reflects a flaw in me. It is a reflection of my lack of patience and sometimes my judgment.

MANTRA: Jehovah El Emeth thank you for revealing my true intentions and lovingly challenging me to do and be better.

Statement of Confession:

_____

_____

_____

_____

_____

_____

_____

_____

_____

_____

_____

#ThriveLife
#Truth
#V2V

Day 25

Now therefore, fear the Lord, serve Him in sincerity and in truth, and put away the gods which your fathers served on the other side of the River and in Egypt. Serve the Lord!
Joshua 24:14NKJV

 02.18.79

MYTH: I am just like my mom/dad (depending on the day and who you ask), and it's just who I am! Some things are just ingrained in me, and I have been this way for 30+ years (look at you, you thought I was going to reveal my age). At this point, I should resign myself to all my characteristics, good, bad and indifferent and people will just have to adjust or be excused. After all, every family comes with their list of issues, and that's just the way life is. The quicker we accept it, the easier we can navigate through life

#ThriveLife
#BreakingGenerationalBondage
#V2V

TRUTH: Who convinced us that we can't change? That is actually a real question. We innately believe we have to wear our generational dysfunction as a badge of honor. It is illogical! We have been changing in every way all our lives (that's a fact), yet somehow we believe we can't change. Our life is a direct contradiction to this belief, and yet we own unhealthy habits that we have learned through generations like if we paid cash for it. Even if you think you paid cash for it, God's word is your receipt with a lifetime warranty. No one keeps a broken product when they have a receipt and a lifetime guarantee. Feel empowered to return those unhealthy traits and get a full refund!

MANTRA: Jehovah Elohim Ab, You are Father of my forefathers; I put off their characteristics and take on Yours.

Statement of Confession:

_____

_____

_____

_____

_____

_____

_____

_____

_____

_____

_____

#ThriveLife
#BreakingGenerationalBondage
#V2V

A man who isolates himself seeks his own desire;
He rages against all wise judgment.
Proverbs 18:1 NKJV

 02.29.68

MYTH: Oh my goodness! As much as I have a sincere love for people, there are many days I wish I were on an island alone. People have become so self-centered and inconsiderate that they just walk all over your desires and needs to get to theirs. I just don't get why society is becoming more self-centered. All this me, me, me (as I write this from *my* perspective all about how *I* feel). No one cares how I feel unless it parallels their feelings and can somehow help them sift through their confusion. Now that we've established that I am also a bit self-centered let's play hide and go seek for a time-out. It's your turn to hide (as I hide also....and pretend to look).

#ThriveLife
#NoFilter
#V2V

TRUTH: Perhaps it feels like people are self-centered and walking all over our needs because our "needs" are in their way. What a thought? Our "needs" may actually be just as stifling to others? Coupled with our ability to filter all our information through our own lenses, and the increased time we spend alone looking at life through our "filters." It is becoming increasingly difficult to understand any point of view that is adverse to our own. We surround ourselves with like-minded people and dismiss other ideas much like the thumbs up/down buttons on all the applications we use. We stay in our comfort zones. As much as we ask "what would Jesus do?" when dealing with others, we are only interested in doing what Jesus did, if it's easy or immediately beneficial. Jesus met people where they are. He served people who you and I would judge and exclude from our circles, but we choose to retreat from others when it becomes uncomfortable.

MANTRA: Jehovah Machsi thank you for being my refuge when my spirit needs to be refueled with silence.

Statement of Confession:

_____
_____
_____
_____
_____
_____
_____
_____
_____
_____
_____

#ThriveLife
#NoFilter
#V2V

Day 27

But we all, with unveiled faces, beholding as in a mirror the glory of the Lord, are being transformed into the same image from glory to glory, just as by the Spirit of the Lord.
II Corinthians 3:18 NKJV

 07.03.71

MYTH: Someone told me I was beautiful and it was very uncomfortable for me to hear. I always get this twinge of discomfort when I hear compliments about my physical attributes. It's always a moment of denial that leads into an awkward "uhm, wow, thank you?" because I don't believe it. Then, I realize the person who complimented me is questioning if they insulted me in some way. Awkward. Especially because many people perceive me to be confident. The confidence they see comes from my intent towards others, not my exterior appearance. I don't see my exterior beauty because I pick apart some of my features and remold them in my mind for a "prettier" version.

#ThriveLife
#Image
#V2V

TRUTH: We spend time admiring and encouraging people about their outer and inner beauty, and spend so much time tearing ourselves down. Somehow we have convinced ourselves that humility equates rejecting the belief that we are beautiful. One does not equate the other, and if we say we are indeed made in God's image, then we are beautiful inside and out!

MANTRA: Elohim, You commanded that Your creation is good; I am Your creation. I believe You

Statement of Confession:

_____
_____
_____
_____
_____
_____
_____
_____
_____
_____
_____
_____

#ThriveLife
#Image
#V2V

Day 28

And the Lord God said, "It is not good that the man should be alone; I will make him a helper comparable to him."
Genesis 2:18

 *1.17.67*

MYTH: I feel weak because I feel lonely. I desire companionship. Believe it or not, I am with a small group of people right now, and I suspect they think I am texting, or posting something on social media about what we are doing. We're all talking, but looking at our "smart" phones. Smartphones have a way of making us look simple; we get together only to communicate with people who are not present about who we're with and what we're pretending to do (since we've already established you're on social media). I have experienced so much loss that I need to connect on a real level. I long for the days of meaningful companionship where there is authentic laughter, sincere exchange of different ideas and opportunities where we challenge growth. I want what many relationships don't seem to offer.

#ThriveLife
#Companionship
#V2V

TRUTH: Feeling lonely and admitting it doesn't make us weak. Companionship is a normal and healthy desire. There is unjustifiable shame in the Christian community in admitting we desire companionship (romantic and otherwise). Admitting you desire and need companionship somehow signals to other people you are not happy with yourself. Again, I would like to remind you, God created us in His own image to love us and for us to love Him. If God sought companionship with us, why is it unnatural for us to desire companionship? In the beginning, everything God created was good; until he referenced Adam being alone – that is the first time God acknowledged something was not good.

MANTRA: God I thank You for sending the right people and relationships my way so I may feel Your presence and authentic connection.

Statement of Confession:

_____

_____

_____

_____

_____

_____

_____

_____

_____

_____

#ThriveLife
#Companionship
#V2V

Day 29

This Book of the Law shall not depart from your mouth, but you shall meditate in it day and night, that you may observe to do according to all that is written in it. For then you will make your way prosperous, and then you will have good success.
Joshua 1:8 KNJV

 05.08.65

MYTH: Someone implied to me that Christians who mediate and/or have mantras are somehow pseudo-Christians. It is not the 1st time I've heard this, and I almost felt the need to defend the practice of meditation and mantras, but I listened. I wanted to understand where the misconception came from. Unfortunately, I still don't know why many Christians believe meditation, mantras, and even yoga are not of God. Interestingly enough, she seems to believe I am a strong Christian. I hope that doesn't change after she reads this work and learns that I am a yoga flexing, meditation practicing and mantra having Christian (gulp).

#ThriveLife
#ChristianMeditation
#V2V

TRUTH: The Bible has many references on meditation. Meditating on scripture and God's promises is truly the only way I have come out of many of my dark moments. I was introduced to yoga and meditation in 2002, and they are some of the best practices I've learned. These practices to quiet our mind, cleanse our spirits and be present, allows us to welcome God into our presence and to feel His peace. Unfortunately, I am no longer in the habit of doing these practices daily, and my stress levels are noticeably different when meditation and yoga are not part of my regular practice. Now that I have my worship nook, my meditations have resumed, and I have been able to do a few yoga practices a month. It has positively impacted my stress levels.

MANTRA: Jehovah Tsemach, make me an extension of you as I meditate on Your word and tree pose (Vrksasana).

Statement of Confession:

_____
_____
_____
_____
_____
_____
_____
_____
_____
_____
_____
_____

#ThriveLife
#ChristianMeditation
#V2V

Day 30

If we claim that we experience a shared life with Him and continue to stumble around in the dark, we're obviously lying through our teeth – we're not living what we claim. But if we walk in the light, God himself being the light, we also experience a shared life with one another, as the sacrificed blood of Jesus, God's Son, purges all our sins.
I John 1: 6-7 MSG

 *07.17.80*

MYTH: I am not going to church today. I will listen to service online and avoid dealing with the hypocrisy. I don't feel like seeing people who speak blessings over my life with an impure heart. They say, "God bless you" in passing with such pretense. I don't need it! I could stay home, get the same word, and not deal with unbelieving believers. Besides, I don't need to be in church to hear from God, and I surely could save on the commute time and get more done with my day.

#ThriveLife
#Fellowship
#V2V

TRUTH: The reality is, we are all sinners (and hypocrites on some level). The very fact that I've had the above thought about my church family and my church attendance screams hypocrisy. These thoughts are not Christ-like; they were laced with elitism and judgment. I too, have extended the fleeting "God bless you's," because I am selfishly consumed with my own desires for a blessing. We are commanded to fellowship with other believers to have accountability. Where I am weak, another believer will be strong and extend support for an upright faith-walk. When we shy away from spiritual fellowship, we deny ourselves the blessings of a biblical support system and accountability.

MANTRA: Jehovah, teach me how to authentically fellowship with Your people in every environment.

Statement of Confession:

_____

_____

_____

_____

_____

_____

_____

_____

_____

_____

_____

_____

_____

#ThriveLife
#Fellowship
#V2V

*"Now, therefore," says the Lord, "Turn to Me
with all your heart, with fasting, with weeping
and with mourning."*
Joel 2:12 NKJV

 09.25.39

MYTH: I did it! I just finished a fast and guess what? I heard clearly, consistently and without contradiction! I feel great, I feel so empowered and ready to concur my challenge. I went before God, and He spoke. I can rest. I even got a prophetic word – more than once! I can let go and give it to God because He's got this. All I needed was for Him to tell me if I am in alignment with His will and confirm the light at the end of the tunnel.

#ThriveLife
#ISubmit
#V2V

TRUTH: I could have released this burden a long time ago! God's answer has not changed, He didn't say anything different during my fast. He literally has been saying the same thing all along. He didn't change – surprise! The difference was in my posture. I was desperately chasing after Him during my fast and not demanding an answer. I submitted my will in exchange for hearing His. I submitted my desires in exchange for bold obedience. I submitted my doubts to receive confirmation. What was different was my willingness to submit every day. God doesn't require that we fast to draw near, He is always with us and speaking to us. However, there is spiritual, emotional and mental overhaul that takes place when you intentionally sacrifice a desire for His glory.

MANTRA: Jehovah El Emeth, thank you for revealing my true intentions and lovingly challenging me to do better and be better.

Statement of Confession:

_____
_____
_____
_____
_____
_____
_____
_____
_____
_____
_____

#ThriveLife
#ISubmit
#V2V

From Victim to Victory

By now, I hope you are aware that this journey was about dispelling the lies you have believed about people, life and most of all, you. The easiest way for the enemy to derail us is by convincing us we are not who God says we are and we are not on that train to victory. Even if you have not been able to erase all the lies you've believed all your life – keep pressing! The only way to live on purpose every day is by feeding your soul with His Word and dwelling in His presence daily. Ask me how I know?

Well, the days I am able to serve and sow seeds for His Kingdom are days that my responses to the challenges of life are different. Notice, I said my response is different, not my circumstances. Believe it or not, those days are filled with peace, sleep, and even joy; true joy. The days I go against my calling and lose focus of my purpose, are days that are filled with menacing thoughts of defeat, sleepless nights and even depression.

The truth is, when you take your mind off of Him and who we truly are in Him, we are leaving our mind open to be Satan's playground. It is a real battle to intentionally protect your mind! Every day I have to make a conscious decision to protect my image in Him! This is still a challenge for me in a few areas, but I am determined to meditate on His promises every day. Let me say it again, we are made in His image, and therefore we are already victorious, we just need to remember to walk in victorious authority - every day!

GLOSSARY

This glossary is provided for you to find your own mantra for each challenge. If you lack the words to say, calling on His name is enough. There is true power in calling His name.

Adonai – Master Over All (Deuteronomy 3:24)

Ehyeh Asher Ehyeh – The eternal, all-sufficient God (Exodus 3:14)

El Bethel – The God of the house of God (Genesis 35:7)

El Elohe Yisrael – The Might God of Israel (Genesis 33:20)

El Elyon – The most high God (Daniel 3:26)

El Emunah – The faithful God (Deuteronomy 7:9)

El Hakabodh – The God of glory (Psalm 29:3)

El Hayyay – God of my life (Psalm 42:8)

El Kanna – Jealous God (Exodus 20:5)

El Nekamoth – God that avengeth (Psalm 18:47)

El Ria – God Who sees me (Genesis 16:13)

El Sali – God my rock (II Samuel 22:47)

El Shaddai – Almighty God (Genesis 17:1-2)

El Simchath Gili – God of my exceeding joy (Psalm 43:4)

Eli Maelekhi – God my King (Psalm 68:24)

Elohe Tishuathi – God of my salvation (Psalm 51:14

Elohe Tsadeki– God of my righteousness (Psalm 4:1)

Elohe Yakob – God of Jacob (Psalm 20:1)

Elohei Chasdi – God of my kindness, goodness & faithfulness (Psalm 59:17)

Elohei Haelohim – God of gods (Deuteronomy 10:17)

Elohei Marom – God of heights (Micah 6:6)

Elohei Ma'uzzi – God of my strength (II Samuel 22:33)

Elohei Mikkarov – God who is near (Jeremiah 23:23)

Elohei Tehillati – God of my praise (Psalm 109:1)

Elohenu Olam – Our everlasting God (Psalm 48:14)

Elohim – The strong Creator (Genesis 1:1-2)

Elohim Bashamayim – God in heaven (Joshua 2:11)

Elohim Chaseddi – God of mercy (Psalm 59:10)

Elohim Chayim – The Living God (Joshua 3:10)

Elohim Kedoshim – Holy God (Joshua 24:19)

Elohim Machase Lanu - God our refuge (Psalms 62:8)

Elohim Ozer Li – God my helper (Psalm 54:4)

Elohim Shophtim Ba-arets – The God who judges the earth (Psalm 58:11)

Elohim Tishuathi – God of my salvation (Psalm 51:14)

Elohim Tsebaoth – God of hosts (Psalm 80:7)

Esh Oklah – A consuming fire (Deuteronomy 4:24)

Immanuel – God Who is with us (Isaiah 7:14)

Jehovah – Master and relational God (Genesis 2:4)

Jehovah Adon Kol Ha-arets – Lord of all the earth (Joshua 3:11)

Jehovah Chereb – The Sword (Deuteronomy 33:29)

Jehovah El Emeth – God of truth (Psalms 31:5)

Jehovah El Gemuwai – God of recompense (Jeremiah 51:56)

Jehovah Elohim Tsaba – The Son of God (Matthew 16:16)

Jehovah Gibbor Milchamah – Might Lord in battle (Psalm 24:8)

Jehovah Goelekh – Redeemer (Isaiah 60:16)

Jehovah Hashopet – The Judge (Judges 11:27)

Jehovah Hoshiah – Victorious God (Psalm 20:9)

Jehovah Immeka – The Lord Who is with you (Judges 6:12)

Jehovah Jireh – Provider (Genesis 22:14)

Jehovah Kanna Shemo – The Lord Whose name is Jealous (Exodus 34:14)

Jehovah Machsi – My refuge (Psalm 91:9)

Jehovah Magen - My Shield (Deuteronomy 33:29)

Jehovah Maginnenu – Lord of our defense (Psalm 89:18)

Jehovah Mauzzi – My Fortress (Jeremiah 16:19)

Jehova Mekaddishkem – The Lord Who Sanctifies (Exodus 31:13)

Jehovah Mephalti – My Deliverer (Psalm 18:2)

Jehovah Metsudhathi – Strong Tower (Psalm 18:2)

Jehovah Moshiekh – The Lord your Savior (Isaiah 49:26)

Jehovah Nissi – My Banner (Exodus 17:15)

Jehova Ori – My Light (Psalm 27:1)

Jehovah Sal'l – My Rock (Psalm 18:2)

Jehovah Shalom – Lord of peace (Judges 6:24)

Jehovah Shammah - Lord Who is always there. (Ezekiel 48:35 NKJV)

Jehova Rohi – The Shepherd (Psalms 23:1)

Jehovah Rophe – Healer (Exodus 15:26)

Jehovah Tsaba – Lord of hosts (I Samuel 17:45)

Jehovah Tsemach – The branch of the Lord (Isaiah 4:2)

Jehovah Tsidkenu – Righteous Lord (Jeremiah 23:6)

'Or Goyim – Light of all nations (Isaiah 42:6)

Peleh Yo'etz – Wonderful Counselor (Isaiah 9:6)

Ruach Hakkodesh – Holy Spirit (Psalm 51:11)

Tony Evans | Teaching Truth. Transforming Lives. Praying (and Pronouncing) the Names of God. May 14, 2015.

ABOUT THE AUTHOR

Born in Tobago – Trinidad & Tobago T.F. Hoskins loves and appreciates her West-Indian heritage. Her upbringing and exposure to diversity has instilled a great appreciation, understanding, and love for people of different cultures and ethnicities.

At a very young age, Hoskins began to show interest in law and had a dream of becoming an attorney. In an effort to fulfill her dream of being an attorney, she began to pursue knowledge in all dimensions; acquiring a Bachelor's Degree in Criminal Justice and a Paralegal Certificate from the Northeastern University. Hoskins' love for academics and passion for law earned her an acceptance by the London School of Law, though she was unable to answer the call, Hoskins went on to receive additional certifications through Harvard's Management Mentor Program along with additional certifications as a Prepare/Enrich Marital Coach. With the acquisition of training and skills, she achieved a milestone in 2008 as she served as the President of the Trinidad and Tobago Association of GA, Inc. She was the first female and the youngest to ever occupy the honorary position, setting standards and by leaving a legacy during her term from 2008 to 2010.

Making a brave move from Boston to Atlanta, Hoskins made the decision to leave her job at the Board of Bar Overseers of Massachusetts, SJC. At the time it was a tough but important decision. She left everything she built and achieved to start all over again in a city (Atlanta) that she visited only once. But little did she know, it was a blessing in disguise.

Later on, Hoskins met her husband, a relationship that brought an entirely new meaning to life. The relationship was fruitful as she and Mr. Hoskins welcomed a son to the family. The birth of their son was the best thing that happened to her; she affectingly refers to them (husband and son) as her M&M's.

Hoskins currently works as a Service Delivery Analyst who manages and performs quality control reviews for over $1 billion dollars of non-qualified accounts held by a major bank.

Although an Author and Life Coach, Hoskins most honorable ministry is being a wife to a caring husband and a mother to her loving son.

Made in the USA
Columbia, SC
14 November 2020